CW00421465

How to Set Up a Tutoring Business

ISBN-13: 978-1479230877

ISBN-10: 1479230871

HOW TO SET UP A TUTORING BUSINESS

Essential Start-Up Tips to Boost Your Tutoring Business Success

Gregory Nollin

I dedicate this book to every person – be they woman or man whose lives have been touched by the dedication and professionalism of a tutor...

Contents

Tutoring Business
An Introduction

You were always good in school and you always helped your friends with their homework.

These days, you're helping your nephews and nieces with theirs.

Why not use your skills to earn extra income on the side?

With very little capital, you can start earning money from the knowledge that you already have.

This kind of work allows you to see other people overcome challenges and attain success in their lives.

It also enables you to help them solve problems and break through barriers such that they're able to realise their true potential.

So, if you feel that you have a lot to give as a person and you possess the unique ability to help others see challenges in a different light, then helping them attain the confidence needed to step forward and grab hold of whatever achievement they're after, this may indeed be the perfect business venture for you.

Regardless of whether you currently hold a full-time job, working part-time, or are a stay-at-home mom, you can still make a success of a tutoring business.

Tutoring sessions are usually done in the evenings primarily because students spend the day at school. You can therefore schedule your sessions a few evenings each week or even on weekends.

One of the major advantages of a home tutoring business is that you get to be very flexible about your work hours. You can choose to do tutoring only two nights each week or maybe only on Saturdays. It's your call, really.

You may not have realised it just yet, but home-based tutoring is actually one of the best ways for you to use your skills while enjoying the various perks of working from home.

In fact, there's currently a serious demand for people with excellent communication and problem solving skills, coupled with empathy, understanding, and a natural love for helping other people.

People like this have been known to accomplish some amazing things both for themselves and the people within their social circle, which may be why they're currently in demand.

You should also realise that tutoring is currently among the fastest-growing home businesses all over the world. And the good news is that there are plenty of options for you to choose from.

You may want to work as a private tutor, an online tutor working for a tutoring agency, a local tutor working for a tutoring centre, or a tutor for students taking distance learning or correspondence classes.

Whatever type of tutoring business you decide to get into, you can surely make a success of it as long as you have a positive mindset.

Qualities you need to be a successful tutor

It takes a very special individual to become a successful tutor. You'll have to be able to teach and coach your students effectively, identify problems in the student's learning process, and then devise and implement a plan of action that'll help your students work through their problems and succeed in whatever it is they're studying.

Here are the four basic traits you need to possess if you're serious about becoming a successful tutor:

1. Being knowledgeable about the subject

It goes without saying, of course, that a good tutor should have extensive knowledge in the subject he plans to teach. It's also advantageous for him to have a significant amount of experience in the subject. This combination of knowledge and experience will be among your greatest assets and advantages when you enter the world of tutoring.

2. Communication skills

Take note that a tutor's job isn't focused solely on teaching the subject.

Aside from being a good teacher or lecturer, you need to be a good listener as well. This is very important in ensuring that you're able to transfer your knowledge effectively to your student. It's expected that a student may sometimes have some learning difficulties and part of your job as a tutor is identifying what's causing these difficulties.

Furthermore, you need to guide your student through the process of overcoming those difficulties. After all, you can't realistically transfer knowledge without breaking through the learning difficulties.

And the best way to identify the barriers to learning is to listen to your student. Your goal in tutoring should always be to empower your student such that he can move on to no longer needing a tutor. That might sound counterproductive, but that's the best measure of your success.

3. Understanding and patience

In a tutoring business, you mostly work one on one. Therefore, you need to understand that each student is an individual with his or her own personality and set of learning needs.

It's very important to exercise a great deal of understanding and patience, especially when a student fails to grasp a concept regardless of how clearly you think you've explained it.

Always bear in mind that the student's knowledge isn't at the same level as yours, so you'll really have to exert extra effort.

Among other things, you need to show your student that you're someone he or she can trust and that you won't lose patience with him or her as he or she battles through the learning difficulties.

4. Ability to develop and implement a plan

As you work with your student, you'll need to constantly look for the areas that are tripping him or her up.

Once you've identified these areas, you need to start making a concrete plan on how to take your student from his or her current knowledge level to the knowledge level you believe he or she can realistically attain.

Being realistic in setting your goals is essential because you need to provide your student with a challenge he or she can aspire to without setting him or her up for disappointment.

With constant practice, you should be able to sharpen your people skills and gain more confidence in your tutoring abilities.

Always remember that your students will most probably be able to tell if you sincerely care about their progress or not. So, before you even launch your tutoring business, make sure you're someone a student can truly look up and relate to.

Here's a quick overview of how to get started:

1. Check with your local school organization to get a general idea of which age group needs help with their studies the most. You may also want to check which particular area in your community needs tutoring services most.

2. Prepare an agreement or a contract for you and your clients to sign. Make sure the agreement outlines all of your expectations, especially as regards payment, terms, and schedules. Outline what you have to offer so your clients will know what to expect as well.

3. Prepare a business plan detailing where you will conduct tutoring sessions and what particular subjects you'll be tutoring on.

4. Advertise your business by inserting fliers into mailboxes and putting up announcements on public bulletin boards. You could also ask family and friends to spread the word about your new business and pass your business cards out to people around your neighbourhood.

5. Purchase fun materials that can help you keep children's interest while you're tutoring. Flash cards, coloured markers and pens, and specialty papers are all good options.

Of course, you should also buy the essentials: textbooks, workbooks, and a computer, among other things.

Finally, learn as much as you can about tutoring so you can improve your services as you go along.

Above all, you should learn to be patient.

It may take some time for people to realize they could make use of your services, but once they do, you're likely to have plenty of business on your hands.

Things to Consider

Private tutoring is indeed a very effective method of learning and an extremely beneficial endeavour for both the tutor and the student.

Managing the logistics of a tutoring business, however, can be a bit challenging, which is why you'll have to seriously assess yourself to determine if this is indeed the career path you'd want to take.

Many professionals entered the world of tutoring simply because they believed in the concept and saw an opportunity to earn good money while doing something they enjoy. Pretty soon, however, they realise this kind of work can take up a good deal of your time if you don't manage it carefully.

What Hours Will You Work?

This is perhaps the first question you should ask yourself once you've decided to do some tutoring work.

Among the best things about a tutoring business is that you get to decide on your own working hours. Of course, the most common schedules for tutoring sessions are in the evenings or on weekends, since students are typically at school during the day on weekdays.

Depending on your own daily schedule, you can decide whether to conduct tutoring sessions on weekends only or each evening from Monday to Friday. You may even want to schedule sessions on the evenings of Mondays through Fridays and also the whole day of Saturday.

In deciding what specific hours you'll hold your tutoring sessions in, what's important is for you to take the schedule of your target clients into account. Always remember that a tutoring business is service-oriented, which makes it important to always consider the client's convenience first.

If you're planning to tutor young kids, for example, they usually get out of school in the early afternoon, so you could begin your sessions by then if you're available.

It's best to discuss the schedule with your students or their parents beforehand so you can work out a schedule that's convenient to both parties.

How Much Tutoring Will You Do Each Week?

Needless to say, how much you earn will depend largely on how many hours you decide to work each week. For starters, you may want to tutor for just three hours each night, Mondays through Fridays.

If you charge $30 per hour, then you'll be earning $450 a week from your tutoring business.

After a few months with this setup, you'd likely be in a much better position to decide whether tutoring is something you'd want to do for the rest of your life. In that case, you can adjust your work hours and hourly rates accordingly.

Once you decide to make tutoring your primary source of income, you can start increasing the number of hours you spend on session each day.

Taking off from the above example, you could perhaps adjust your schedule to go from three hours a day to six, with each session lasting two hours. You can therefore take on three students each day. This gives you ample time to spend with your family or on other personal endeavours.

And if you maintain your original rate of $30 per hour, you could earn $900 a week if you work only from Mondays through Fridays. If you hold sessions on Saturdays, then you earn $180 more each week.

The beauty of a tutoring business lies in the way you can tailor your work schedule around your personal responsibilities and social activities.

If you're a mother, for example, you could schedule your tutoring sessions when your kids are at school, asleep, or otherwise engaged so you don't get interrupted.

If you're a college student looking for extra cash, then you can schedule tutoring sessions when you don't have classes or extra-curricular activities.

If you're a career woman and you're not quite ready to let go of your day job just yet, then you can schedule tutoring sessions after work.

Tutoring Regulations?

Just like any other business venture, you'll need to find out what the rules and regulations are in your country where a tutoring business is concerned.

After all, you wouldn't want to set up a tutoring business and then get into trouble with the law just when you're enjoying the work immensely and earning good money from it, right?

Another huge advantage to knowing the rules that govern your business is that it enables you to address any questions or concerns your would-be clients might have when you first explain your business and try to sell your services to them.

How Much Should You Charge?

When getting into the tutoring business, you'll need to know how much you can charge your clients. Sure, the main thing is for you to have a passion for teaching and helping others. But, it is still a business after all and you'll need to earn enough to make the effort worth your while.

Remember that charging too little can make your service appear weak, while charging too much can drive potential customers away, especially if you're just starting out.

So, just how much can you realistically charge your clients for a tutoring session?

The amount you earn from a tutoring business will depend largely on whether you work for someone else or own the business.

As an employee, you're likely to receive a fixed hourly pay, which is typically a percentage of the hourly rates charged by the tutoring company you work for. For example, if the company you work for charges $50 per hour, you're likely to get about $10-$15 per hour as your salary.

If you established your own tutoring business, though, you earn what you charge for the most part. For example, if you charge $50 per hour, then you earn $50 per hour.

Of course, you'll have to deduct the cost of advertising, book-keeping, and other expenses in order to determine what your net income is.

What's important is for you to find out what the current average rate in the market is and then base your charges on that figure.

The current average rate is pegged at $20 per hour and you can decide to go a bit lower or higher than that, depending on how much value you place on your work and how much experience you have in tutoring.

If you can justify going as high as $50 per hour, then by all means, charge that rate.

Once you've decided exactly how much you're going to charge your students, you'll have to decide on the billing period as well.

Are you going to require payment immediately after each session or do you prefer to collect payment on a monthly basis?

For many people in the tutoring business, weekly payments are ideal. Whatever decision you arrive at, make sure you discuss the terms clearly with your clients right at the outset.

It's also advisable to buy a receipt book and invoice book to use for billing and collecting payment from your clients.

Make sure the books you buy copy in triplicate so you can give a copy to your client, keep a copy for yourself, and then keep an extra copy in your files in case a client loses his copy and wants another.

Keeping your copy in the book and tearing out only the one you give to your client is a good idea. It's also advisable to always keep your invoices and receipts properly matched up and in good order so as to keep your financial records well-organized.

Should you decide to sign up with an online tutoring agency, you're likely to be given the freedom to set your own pay rates. In this case, the decision as to how much your time is worth rests on you alone. You may want to browse the agency's website and check how much other tutors are charging.

Ultimately, though, the rate you charge should be based on the value you place on your services. More than anything else, you should remember to never, ever sell yourself short.

Now let's get down to some business specifics.

Naming Your Tutoring Business

Choosing a company name can be the most fun part of starting a company. It can also be one of the most important.

After all, having the right tutoring business name can be a very effective advertising tool. Among other things, it can give prospective customers a general idea of what your company does and what you have to offer. In the same way, choosing the wrong name is likely to drive would-be customers away.

Here are a couple of things to remember when choosing a tutoring business name:

1. Keep it short and memorable

Needless to say, a short company name is much easier to remember than a lengthy one.

Choosing a short name doesn't just involve using less words, but also words with less syllables.

But, aside from being short, your tutoring business name also has to be catchy so as to promote better name recall.

2. You are your name

This means your company name should reflect the company's personality.

It should give people a general idea of what services you provide or what benefits they can get from patronizing your tutoring business.

You need to have an image which you want your tutoring business to project and the name you choose must fit that image.

More importantly, you have to choose a name your target customers can easily connect with.

Now, you know the basics of choosing a company name and you realize how important a name is to your business.

However, you shouldn't take the process of choosing a name too seriously.

While the company name does have to reflect its personality, it doesn't really have to define your company completely.

Take note that venturing into other related businesses is a normal part of any company's growth, so there is a real possibility that you may have to change your tutoring business name from time to time.

Again, the name of your tutoring business is important, but you shouldn't get hung up on the process of choosing it.

As long as you make sure that it's memorable, it tells people what your tutoring business is about, and you're proud of it, then you're good to go.

Developing a new tutoring business naturally requires a good foundation, and building such a foundation begins with having a sound business plan.

Remember that the business plan is an essential part of documenting a start-up business' financial goals, business objectives, and marketing plans.

Implementation of all your tutoring business ideas can only successfully begin once you've completed your business plan.

Your Business Plan: Choosing the Right Format

You probably already know that a business plan ranks among the most vital components of starting your tutoring business and ensuring its success.

But, how exactly do you make a good business plan? Well, there are several variations and templates you can choose from. What's important is for you to choose the one that's best suited to the kind of enterprise you'll be running and to the purpose for which you're making the plan in the first place.

Here are some of the things you need to take into consideration:

1. Your Target Audience

There are two types of business plan.

a. There are business plans intended for an internal audience and these plans are usually part of your tutoring business growth strategy; they're also usually referred to as strategic plans.

b. There are also plans meant for external audiences and the purpose of these plans is usually to attract financing, suppliers, or talent for your tutoring business. If the purpose of your business plan is primarily to get funding, then the document will typically be in condensed form, or a sort of summary of a more comprehensive business plan.

Such a version is generally known as a *funding proposal* or a *business opportunity document* and it's usually followed by the larger plan.

A business plan can indeed be a very useful document, so it's important to clearly define the audience for which it is intended.

2. What Goes Into the Plan?

Remember that a business plan needs to be comprehensive and that it's essentially created to put into writing what you envision for your tutoring business venture.

Your tutoring business plan should contain:

- An executive summary
- The background and history of your company
- A clear description of your tutoring business concept
- Your marketing analysis and development plan
- Your operations and production assessment
- Your financial assessments and projections
- Your resources management assessment and plan
- Your business implementation plan
- An identification of resources
- The investor deal structures wherever appropriate
- A survival strategy that describes potential risks
- Your tutoring business growth strategy
- Your exit strategy
- Appendices

If that seems daunting, don't worry.

Some of the components of your business plan may be longer than others and some of them are optional, depending on your target audience, the format you choose to adopt, and the purpose of your plan.

What's important is for your intended reader to clearly grasp the value proposition, understand why your tutoring business is expected to succeed, and how that success will be achieved.

If you're pitching the plan to potential investors, (or most probably the bank) then they should quickly understand your proposed deal structure and the possible returns.

3. What Length To Make Your Plan

The average business plan typically consists of 20 pages, though there are some that contain a hundred pages or more. The length of your plan will depend largely on its purpose and your target audience.

If the primary purpose of your business plan is to attract investors, then you can expect it to contain more details and therefore be lengthier than a plan that's primarily for communicating your tutoring business growth strategy. In the same way, the business plan for a venture with a relatively simple concept should be a lot more concise than one that's made for a highly complicated enterprise.

4. Should You Use a Template or Pay a Consultant?

Many people are also confused as to whether they should hire a consultant to help them write their business plan or simply use a template for guidance. Well, it can be quite tempting to use a template or get someone else to make the plan for you.

However, it's still best if you write the plan yourself even if you do decide to get some guidance from a consultant. After all, who knows your business better than you?

A solid business plan is perhaps the easiest way for you to communicate your tutoring business ideas to your target audience as well as to help you prevent problems and identify business growth strategies. It can also be your most valuable tool when you're in search of funding for your tutoring business.

Remember, though, that instead of treating it as a blueprint or a strict manual which you should implement to the letter, the plan should be seen as more of a guide in operating your tutoring business.

TIP: Even if you don't have an immediate audience for your plan, the document and even the process itself will definitely prove to be of value to your business in the long run.
Preparing a solid business plan for all the right reasons can indeed increase your chances of attaining success in your tutoring business.

Your Business Plan – How to Write the Executive Summary

The executive summary generally serves as the introduction to your formal and comprehensive business plan.

You could even say that this is Part 1 of your business plan.

It contains a summary of your tutoring business proposition, present business status, financial projections, and the key elements for success.

Although it's often tempting to just rush through this component of your business plan, always remember that an executive summary is likely to be the very first thing your target investors or banking officials will read in the document.

It basically tells the reader the status of the company currently, and where it's expected to go. Many people aren't likely to read the remainder of the plan if the executive summary doesn't catch their interest, so it's really very important to do this right.

The importance of the executive summary lies in the fact that it tells your reader exactly why you believe your tutoring business will be a success.

Brevity is the key to a solid executive summary, which generally ranges from half a page to a maximum of two pages.

Writing anything longer puts you at risk of losing the reader's attention and appearing unfocused. If you can keep the summary under one page without sacrificing quality, then do so.

Note: Although it serves as the introduction, it's best to write the executive summary after you've completed your business plan. After all, it is basically a shorter version of your plan.

To keep the summary consistent with the plan itself, it should have the following components:

1. Your Mission Statement

Your business plan's executive summary is be the best place for you to express your mission statement. Make sure that statement is concise and explains in as few words as possible the existence of your tutoring business, its goals, and how you plan to achieve those goals.

In short, it should explain your tutoring business thrust to the reader. Remember to keep your mission statement focused and direct, leaving no room for confusion as regards what your tutoring business venture is all about.

2. What's Your Business Concept?

In describing your tutoring business concept, you'll need to offer some details about the kind of tutoring business you'll be running, who your target customers are, and what your competitive advantages are.

You may point out that you're filling a void you've identified in the market, offering better prices for comparable services in the industry, or offering a better service than what's currently available.

3. A Little Background

You may also want to give your reader an idea of when your venture began, who the founders are and what functions they perform, how many employees you have (or plan to hire), and where the tutoring business is located and if there are any subsidiaries or branches. A description of your offices and facilities as well as the services your offer would also be a good idea.

4. Your Tutoring Business Status and Financial Outlook

You'll also need to give a short description of the current status of your tutoring business. Explain if your business is still in the conceptualization stage, if you've already started setting it up, or if it's already fully operational and you're simply planning to expand.

You should also mention your expected costs and your financial projections for both the short term and the long term.

This will give potential investors an idea of how much capital you need and if your business venture matches the kind of opportunity they're currently looking for. If you already have existing investors, then you'd do well to provide some information on them as well.

5. Key Factors for Success

The reader of your business plan will also appreciate getting a preview of the key factors for tutoring business success. These factors depend on your situation, of course, but it generally includes technology patents, strategic partnerships, market factors and economic trends.

If your tutoring business is already fully operational and you've had some successful projects worth noting (you may have been the first to offer a certain service in the industry), then you should include that as well.

Finally...

All in all, your business plan's executive summary should provide its reader with a quick but insightful glimpse into the plan itself.

It's advisable to highlight everything except the mission statement in bulleted lists. Include all of the important points without revealing too much, since each section is discussed in detail within the plan itself, anyway.

More importantly, make sure the summary sells the proposal on its own as much as possible, just in case reader doesn't read your plan. It does happen!

Note: It's also a good idea to draw up a table of contents right after the executive summary so the reader will know where he can find each section in the plan itself.

If you're still in the process of setting up your tutoring business, then you likely won't have much to write as regards to some of the areas listed above.

In that case, focus on your own experience and expertise in the field, and the circumstances that led to your tutoring business concept.

Tell your target readers how you plan to set your tutoring business apart from the competition and convince them that there's indeed a need for your business within your target niche or industry.

Your Business Plan – Company History

After the executive summary, your business plan should contain a section covering your business background or company history. The length of this portion and how it's told will depend largely on how far along your tutoring business is in terms of operations and development.

Naturally, the business history of a venture that's just starting is totally different from one that's been operating for some time. It should be about one page long, though it's understandable for a start-up company's history to cover less than an entire page.

What to Include

In this section, you should be able to illustrate how the various elements of your tutoring business venture fit together and form one successful enterprise.

You should also include some background information on the nature of the tutoring business itself and identify the factors that are expected to facilitate its success. Furthermore, don't forget to mention the specific market needs you're planning to satisfy and the ways and methods in which you expect to satisfy these needs. If possible, you should also identify the specific individuals or groups of people whom you believe have those needs.

An example of a specific market could be:

Parents aged 20 to 35 with an income of $80,000 within 50 miles of your location.

How It All Started

Among the things you should include in the company history portion of your business plan is the origin of your tutoring business concept.

This explains how you first came upon the idea for your tutoring business and why you decided to pursue that idea. You should also indicate the progress you've made so far as regards operating and growing your business venture. If you're still in the process of starting your business, then say so.

NOTE: It's also a good idea to mention the problems you've encountered along the way and how you handled each of them. Potential investors and business partners will surely appreciate knowing that they're dealing with someone who's not afraid to deal with challenges from time to time.

Projected Short-Term Growth

You would also do well to include your short-term business growth plans in this section, so the reader will know that you've thought about your venture carefully and that you have concrete plans for its growth.

NOTE: If you're just starting a new tutoring business, then you may want to include a bit of personal history along with your background.

Among the things you can include are your educational history, technical skills, areas of expertise, relevant professional club memberships, and other tutoring businesses you may have started or companies you worked for.

You may even want to share your areas of inexperience or weaknesses and how you intend to compensate for these areas. Your target investors would definitely appreciate knowing that you're aware of the things you need to improve on and are making concrete efforts at improving them.

Finally...

In summary, the company history section of your business plan should provide an interested reader with a much better idea of how your tutoring business came to be and who you are as a businessperson. Again, the key is to keep this section concise and avoiding unwanted information.

Your Business Plan – Organization and Management

This section of your plan includes the following:
- Your company's organizational structure

- The profiles of your management team

- Details about company ownership

- The board of director's qualifications

It's important for you to answer the question of who does what when you prepare this section.

Explain what each person's background and qualifications are. Tell your reader exactly why you've brought or are bringing these people into your organization and management team.

What exactly are they responsible and accountable for?

NOTE: You may think this section of the plan is unnecessary if you're setting up a small venture with less than five people on your team, but anybody reading your business plan needs to know who's in charge. Therefore, you should still provide a description of every department or division, along with their functions, regardless of the size of your company.

If there's an advisory board for your business, then you should also identify who's on it and how you plan to keep each member on the board.

- What salary and benefits do you plan to provide for members of your team?

- Will you be offering incentives? If so, what are they?

- How do you plan to handle promotions?

In this section of your business plan, you need to reassure your audience that the people on your team aren't going to be just names on your company letterhead.

What's Your Structure?

One very simple yet effective way of presenting your organizational structure is by creating an organizational chart and then providing a narrative description of the chart.

By doing this, you don't leave anything to chance, you're making sure the functions and responsibilities of each team member has been carefully thought out, and you've ensured that someone's in charge of each and every function in your tutoring business. Therefore, no function is taken for granted and there'll be no overlapping of responsibilities.

TIP: Remember that this kind of assurance is very important to your reader, especially if that reader is a potential investor.

Management Profiles

Ask any business expert and he'll probably tell you that among the most significant success factors in any business is the track record and ability of the management team.

This is why it's important for you to provide your reader with a background of the key members of the management team.

Specifically, you'd do well to provide resumes that indicate the name, position and the corresponding functions, primary responsibilities and level of authority, educational background, skills and experience, number of years on your team (unless it's a start-up company), compensation level and basis, previous employment and track record, industry recognitions received, and community involvement.

When you indicate the track record of your team, be sure to quantify their achievements.

For example, instead of saying:

"Extensive experience in managing a sales department"

you could say:

"Successfully managed a sales department of ten people for 15 years."

It's also a good idea to highlight how the key members of the management team complement your own experience and expertise.

If you're starting a new tutoring business, then show your reader how the unique experiences of each member of your team can contribute to your business venture's overall success.

Company Ownership

Aside from the organizational structure, this section of the plan should also describe the legal structure and provide important ownership information regarding your tutoring business.

- Has the business been incorporated? If so, then is it an S or a C corporation?

- Is your business a partnership?

- If so, then is it a limited or general partnership?

- Or are you the sole proprietor of your tutoring business?

The most important pieces of information you should include in this section are the owner/s' names, ownership percentage, form of ownership, degree of involvement of each owner within the business and outstanding equity equivalents.

Board Qualifications

Take note that there's a huge advantage to setting up an unpaid board of advisors for your company, as it can provide you with the kind of expertise the company is otherwise unable to afford.

Simply by enlisting the help of some successful businessmen who are popular in the industry and including them in your advisory board, you'll definitely go far in enhancing the credibility of your company and encouraging a perception of expertise.

If the company has a board of directors, then you need to provide the names of the board members, their respective positions in the BOD, their background, the extent of their involvement with the tutoring business, and their expected contribution to its success.

Market Analysis

You may be a hundred percent confident about the quality of the service your tutoring business has to offer, but unless you're able to connect with your target customers, quality won't do you much good. You'll have to get your service into your customers' hands, so to speak, to get the necessary sales. And that's why you need market analysis. This section of your business plan should be used to illustrate your knowledge of the industry. You may also use it to present highlights and conclusions from the marketing research data you've collected. For your analysis to be reliable, you need to study the three Cs of marketing:

1. Company

2. Customer

3. Competition

Of course, it's understandable that you should be aware of your company's strengths and weaknesses, but you should also know the same things about your competitors so you'll get a better idea of how to deal with them.

More importantly, you need to know who your customers are and what their needs and wants really are. When you prepare the company analysis component of this section, you'll need to describe the primary industry to which your business belongs, the industry's current size and historic growth rate, the industry's characteristics and trends, and the industry's major customer groups.

All these will put into perspective the description you'll provide of the company you've established or are planning to establish.

Who Are Your Target Customers?

In choosing and defining your target customers, make sure that you narrow it down to a size that you're sure you can manage.

Many business owners make the mistake of trying to provide everything to everybody at once. Slow and sure is often a better philosophy where your business is concerned.

This section of your plan should include information that identifies the unique characteristics of your target customers including:

- Their needs

- The extent to which these needs are being met

- Demographics.

It's also a good idea to identify your target market's geographic location, who among them makes the major decisions, and any market trends that may affect your business.

The size of your target market should also be indicated in this section, along with your expected market share gains and the reason for these expected gains.
You should also indicate your pricing schedule as well as your gross margin targets and whatever discount structures you may be planning.

You'd also do well to identify what resources you plan to use to get information as regards your target market, the media you'll be using to reach the market, your target market's purchasing cycle, and the socio-economic trends likely to affect your target market.

If all this sounds complicated don't worry, just break down each section and do it one at a time.

Your Competition

Of all the Cs you need to study, your competition may be the toughest, especially if you're new to the industry. The first thing you need to do is study your direct competitors.

If you're planning to operate a tutoring business in your district, then you're likely to get direct competition from the likes of the larger multi-national tutoring businesses. So it pays to examine all the possible options on how you can set your tutoring business apart.

It's important for you to identify your direct competitors according to product or service line and market segment.

You should then assess their weaknesses and strengths, determine the level of importance of your own target market to your competitors, and identify the barriers that may pose a challenge as you enter your target niche. This may include high investment costs, changing technology, existing patents or trademarks, customer resistance, and a difficulty in finding quality personnel. You'd also do well to determine the market share of each key competitor and then provide an estimate of the time it'll take for new competitors to enter the niche.

Aside from looking for ways to set yourself apart from the competition, you'll also want to see how your business fits into the marketplace itself. In doing so, you'll have to consider the strengths and weaknesses of your competitors, the possibility of competitors leaving the marketplace and new ones entering it, the services your competitors are relying on for a majority of their revenue, and effective ways of overcoming possible threats from substitute services.

Developing Your Marketing Strategy

Once all three Cs have been addressed, you should be ready to start developing your marketing program. This basically involves an analysis of what's known as the "four Ps."

They are:

1. Product

2. Place

3. Price

4. Promotion

Product, of course, refers to what you plan to sell (in this case your tutoring service) Place refers to where you plan to sell it (office, online, or both).

Price refers to the amount you'll charge for each service you'll be offering.

And Promotion refers to the incentives and other promotional strategies you plan to use in order to get your target market to try your services.

To put it simply, a marketing strategy is your way of drawing in customers, which is indeed very important since customers are essentially the lifeblood of any business venture.

There isn't a single way of approaching a marketing strategy. What's important is for your strategy to be uniquely applicable to your tutoring business and part of a continuing evaluation process that aims to facilitate business growth and success. In conducting a "four Ps" analysis, you'll likely conduct some market tests and you'd do well to include the results of these tests in this section of your business plan. All other details of the tests may be attached as an appendix.

The information you provide in this section may include the number of customers who participated in the tests, demonstrations or any information provided to the participating customers, the degree of importance of satisfying the needs of your target market, and the percentage of participants who expressed desire to take advantage of your products and/or services.

After creating your marketing strategy, you'll also need to draw up a sales strategy, which outlines the methods you'll be using to actually sell the services you plan to offer.

There are two very important elements of a good sales strategy.

- The first is your sales force strategy, which determines if you'll be employing internal sales personnel or independent representatives. You should also identify the number of people you plan to recruit for your company's sales force as well as the recruitment and training strategies you'll be using. You'd also do well to present the compensation packages you've lined up for your sales personnel.

- The second element of a sales strategy is a description of the sales activities you've lined up for the company.

A sales strategy is made more manageable when broken down into activities.

For example, you could start with identifying prospective customers and then prioritizing your prospects according to those who have the highest potential of buying your products.

From this outline of activities, you can easily determine the number of prospects you may have to get to make a sale and the average amount you'll likely earn from each sale.
You'll also need to draw up a solid market development plan in order to make your market analysis work to your advantage.

While the information in your development plan is likely to come into play only when your company has been established and operational for at least a few years, potential investors will surely appreciate the fact that you've already envisioned your company's growth and evolution.

Among other things, your development plan should provide answers to the following questions:

> ➢ Is the market for the services you offer currently growing?

> ➢ Are you planning to offer line extensions or new services within your first few years of operations?

> ➢ Does the market development plan you've crafted offer ways of increasing the overall demand for your services within the industry?

> ➢ Are there alternative ways of making your company more competitive?

Remember that the market analysis is a vital part of your business plan and it's likely to take up a large part of the plan itself.

This is why it's necessary to conduct a thorough research on the competition and on the market you're planning to enter.

Finally...

You may have the best service in the market, but without an organized and well-crafted market analysis and development plan, you still won't be able to guarantee success. You market analysis helps you identify a clear roadmap of how to bring your services to your target customers.

Financial Projections

Making financial projections for a start-up tutoring business can be described as both science and art. Investors may want to see you spell out financial forecasts in cold, hard numbers, but it's not really that easy to predict the financial performance of your tutoring business several years from now, especially if you're still in the process of raising capital.

Simply put, this is the part where you formally request funding from potential investors and you do that by illustrating how much funding you need for start-up as well as within the first five years of operations.

If you already have an existing business and are looking towards expansion, then you may reflect the funding requirements for the expansion itself.

Potential investors are also sure to appreciate some historical data as regards the financial performance of your company, particularly within the last three years or so, depending on how long you've been in business.

If you have any collateral that can possibly be used to secure a loan, then that's worth noting as well.

Difficulty aside, financial projections are requirements for a solid business plan and you'll really have to deal with them if you truly want to catch your prospective investors' attention. Regardless of whether your business is a start-up or a growing venture, you'll still need to provide historical and/or projected financial data.

Here are a few useful tips:

1. **Don't let spreadsheets intimidate you**

All financial projections necessarily start with spreadsheet software, with Microsoft Excel being the most commonly used; chances are great you already have the software on your computer. Other than this, there are also some special software packages that can help you with financial projections. These packages often provide flexibility, which allows you to weigh alternate scenarios or change assumptions quickly whenever necessary.

2. **Create short-term projections as well as medium-term projections**

Specifically, your prospective investors should see financial projections for the first year of operations, broken down into monthly projections.

You should also provide a three-year financial projection that's broken down into yearly projections and a five-year financial projection.

TIP: It's advisable, however, to keep your five-year projection separate from your business plan, but readily available in case a potential investor asks to see it.

When you project business growth, be sure to consider the current state of your market, trends in labour and costs, and the possibility of needing additional funding for future expansion.

3. Make sure start-up fees are accounted for

Never forget to include fees for permits, licenses, and equipment in your short-term projections.

You should also keep the difference between variable and fixed costs in mind when making your projections and differentiate between the two wherever necessary. Variable costs are usually placed under the "costs for goods sold" category.

4. Go beyond your income statement

While your income statement is the basic measuring tool by which projected expenses and revenue can be conveyed, a solid financial projection will go beyond that to include projected balance sheets that show a breakdown of your assets, liabilities, and equity, among other things.

You'd also do well to include cash flow projections that reveal cash movement through the company within a given period.

Estimates of the amount you plan on borrowing as well as expected interest payments on those loans should also be included.

Furthermore, you should make sure your financial projections are all in accordance to the GAAP.

TIP: If you're new to financial reporting or don't understand the last paragraph, then you may want to consider hiring an accountant to review your projections.

5. **Offer two scenarios only**

Although you need to go beyond the simple income statement, remember that where financial projections are concerned, potential investors really want to see only two scenarios: The best- and worst-case scenarios. Anything more than those two are superfluous and may just cause unnecessary confusion, so skip it.

Finally...

To sum up, this section should tell potential investors how much money you need now and in the near future, your preferred type of funding and terms, and how you intend to use the funds.

NOTE: Take note that the intended use of the funds is a vital piece of information for potential investors and would-be creditors, which is why you need to explain it in this section.

It's also important to include all pertinent business-related information that can possibly affect the future financial situation of your company. A trend analysis for your financial statements is also very helpful, especially if you present it with graphs, as this is easier to see.

TIP: Above all, you should strive to make reasonable and clear assumptions.

As previously mentioned, financial forecasting is both a science and an art. You'll need to make several assumptions, but you'll also have to be realistic when making those assumptions. Going overboard will likely raise red flags for potential investors, so always make sure your projections are backed up by solid research.

Calculating Your Start-up Costs

What are start-up costs?

These are the expenses you have to deal with before your new tutoring business can actually begin operations and earn revenue.

The concept of start-up costs is very important in tax law because these costs are not considered as deductible expenses, unlike most of the other business costs. You will, instead, need to amortize these costs over the course of a few months or years.

This means you'll only be able to deduct part of the start-up costs each year.

And you can only determine and take full deduction on your other expenses after you have determined start-up costs.

The first step

The first step in calculating the start-up costs of your business is to gather all of the expense receipts from business-related transactions.

Next, determine the exact date when your tutoring business opened and then separate the receipts into two piles: one pile for the expenses from before your business opened and another pile for expenses incurred after the opening day.

The next step is to remove all of the receipts for items such as research costs, taxes, and deductible interest from the pile receipts before opening day.

These costs can immediately be deducted.

Finally, add together all the remaining receipts belonging to your "before opening date" pile. The sum is your total start-up costs, which have to be amortized.

Amortization is usually set over a period of 18 months, and expenses like hiring and training costs, pre-opening advertising, and travel expenses to meet potential suppliers are usually included in the amortized start-up costs.

How to Obtain Business Grants

When starting a business there can be some huge barriers standing in your way, among the biggest of which are start-up costs and other business-related expenses.

You may be planning to take out a loan for the purpose of starting your tutoring business.

Why don't you consider applying for grants from the government or from private organizations instead? There are several reasons why grants are better than a loan, the most obvious of which is the fact that grants don't need to be repaid.

How exactly can you obtain a business grant and turn your simple idea into a thriving tutoring business?

Read on to find out. The Catalog of Federal Domestic Assistance is a good place for you to search for a specific grant you can apply for because it contains a list of all grants available for small tutoring businesses.

The catalog also indicates what type of business qualifies for a particular grant, so you can immediately determine which grants your tutoring business is likely to qualify for.

Another option is for you to visit the Small Business Administration's website, which promotes federal grant programs that offer almost $2 billion to small businesses, particularly those focusing on providing technological solutions to existing business issues.

Once you have identified the grant programs you will be applying for, you should start preparing a business plan.

Take note that grant organizations base their approval or rejection of your application on the contents of your tutoring business plan.

- Your plan should therefore include a statement of purpose that is clearly written and effectively defines the goals of your company.

- A good tutoring business description, an outline of your short-term and long-term goals, a discussion on planned marketing strategies, and a projected financial analysis should also be part of your plan.

The financial section of your plan is very important because organizations usually measure the worth of a candidate based on how you plan to use the grant money.

You should therefore make sure that your financial analysis and hypothetical budget are both conservative and realistic.

When your tutoring business plan is complete, it's time to create your actual grant proposal.

If you have previous experience in creating such a proposal, then you can save some money by writing the proposal yourself.

However, if you've never written a grant proposal before, then it would be wise to hire the services of a professional writer.

Make sure your proposal includes schematics, reports, and some basic information on planned projects that are likely to be influenced by the grant funds.

Furthermore, grant reviewers are likely to appreciate such attention to detail, which may be seen as a strong commitment to your product.

In this case, the reviewers will be more likely to approve your applying for grant funds.

Complete your grant application by including an updated list of contacts.

This list should start with the contact details of the top-level employees.

It should also include the contact details of individuals who can provide important details on the supplementary materials included in your application. Make sure that all pertinent information on your tutoring business and requested files by the grant organization are included in your application.

If your application lacks any of these files, then the grant is likely to be denied or the processing could be very slow. Submit your application only when you're sure that it's complete.

It's also a good idea to have your grant application reviewed by family, friends, and colleagues so grammatical errors can be cleared up and anything you may have overlooked can be pointed out to you.

And as a final review process, you should schedule a reading session together with your staff, so you can correct any identified problems.

Above all, you should be patient.

Take note that the process of getting approved for grants may take longer to complete than the process of getting approved for loans.

This is because grant applications are reviewed a number of times and most grant organizations have to go through thousands of applications at a time.

Getting Insurance for Your Tutoring Business

So, you have an idea for a good tutoring business venture; you even have the name for your new tutoring business already.

And you've also proceeded to create a business plan and a proposal for a grant application.

What else do you need to do prior to actually operating your tutoring business?

You will need good insurance.

This is actually one of the most important steps you need to take when starting a tutoring business. The good news is that there are lots of great places where you can get good advice on the different types of insurance that you may need for your new tutoring business.

An insurance agent is probably the best person for you to approach if you're looking for advice on getting insurance for your tutoring business.

More specifically, you should hire the services of an agent for an insurance company that specializes on tutoring business insurance rather than a general insurance company.

You have to understand that you'll be dealing with a totally different set of risks and challenges with a business than you would with a car or with your home.

Getting insurance from a company that specializes in tutoring business insurance assures you that the agent you're dealing with really knows what he's talking about.

You can expect the insurance agent to lay out several different insurance options for you.

These options can range from liability insurance for your tutoring business to auto insurance.

You may also be offered property insurance as well as loss of business coverage, which protects your interests in case a fire breaks out and you end up without a business to run for a month or so.

It's important for you to ask questions and make sure you understand what each type of insurance covers you for so you can be sure to make an informed decision as to which types of insurance you're going to get.

More often than not, you'll be presented with more insurance options than you can afford.

There's also a possibility that the insurance agent you're consulting will present you with more insurance options than your business actually needs.

This makes it even more important for you to understand what each type of insurance covers. Furthermore, the start of a business is usually a time when you will have to take a few risks by taking out less insurance than your tutoring business needs.

You'll have to decide how much you can afford to spend for insurance and which type of insurance is the most needed by your tutoring business.

Once you've determined this, you can leave the other types of insurance for later.
Most tutoring businesses start only with loss of business coverage, others with liability insurance.
The point is to get only the most important insurance coverage that you can afford for starters. As your company grows, it will become more important for you to protect your tutoring business' assets.

And the good news is that you may able to afford it at that time.

Aside from the insurance that you have previously identified as a need for your tutoring business, there may also be other types of insurance that your customers expect you to have.

You can work on getting these additional insurance types when the right time comes.

How to Trademark Your
Business Name and Logo

If you have just set up a new tutoring business, you should be careful not to stop at choosing a name and logo for it.

You should also make sure that the name and logo you chose is adequately protected.

This is especially important if one of your business goals is to create an instantly recognizable brand. The best way to protect your business name and logo is to have it trademarked.

Take note that a trademark is also used to protect symbols, drawings, and any other character associated with your tutoring business, much like a patent protects inventions.

The whole process of getting your business name and logo trademarked is a relatively simple one. However, it often takes several months for your trademark registration to really become official.

Following is a quick guide on how you can protect your business name and logo by getting it trademarked.

1. Choose the name and design the logo for your new tutoring business.

    You have to make sure, of course, that the name and logo you choose are not yet being used by any other company.

More importantly, you need to ensure that such name and logo have not already been trademarked by someone else.

You can check the database of the official trademark office to make sure you won't run into any legal problems with your chosen name and logo.

2. Once you have established that your chosen tutoring business name and logo are not yet trademarked, request for and fill-out the necessary paperwork.

   Once the paperwork has been filled out and submitted to the Patent and Trademark Office, the processing of your application for registration will officially begin.

3. Allow five months for the processing to be completed.

   If five months have passed and you still have not received any notification of your trademark having been filed, you may check on its status. Take note, though, that it usually takes between five and seven months for a trademark registration process to be completed.

4. Once you receive notification of your trademark having been filed, obtain a copy of it from the trademark office.

Take note that you will be asked for your registration number when you make the request for a copy of your trademark certificate.

5. Between the fifth and sixth year of your trademark registration, make sure that an "Affidavit of Use" is filed, so as to prevent other companies from using your trademarked name and logo.

    You should remember to file two other affidavits as well before every 10-year period of owning the trademark has passed.

Writing an LLC
Operating Agreement

Limited Liability Corporation, or LLC, is the ideal set-up for start-up companies and small businesses because it requires the business owner to take on only limited liability for the company.

And the good news is that creating an LLC is fairly simple and inexpensive. Take note that the operations of an LLC are governed by the LLC operating agreement.

You'll therefore need to learn how to write your LLC operating agreement.

Here is a step-by-step guide:

1. Gather basic information such as the company name and location as well as the names and physical addresses of the members of your company. You should also note your agent's name.

2. Gather all financial information.

   This includes each member's initial contribution to the company and how much each of them will own in terms of percentage of company interest. You can choose to have either a single-member or multi-member LLC.
   For example, you could choose to initially make a contribution of $100 and own a hundred percent of the company.

What's important is for all company members to be included in your LLC operating agreement.

3. Choose and download a sample agreement.

    Of course, you can choose to write your own agreement from scratch, but working from a sample would definitely make the process much easier for you.

    While operating agreements aren't really that complex, the language used can be very governmental, and basing your agreement on a sample will help ensure that the language is interpreted correctly.

4. Determine if you need the services of a registered agent.

    Take note that there's a slight difference in the LLC laws of each state.
    The operating agreement typically has a space that needs to be filled in for the registered agent. If your state's requirements allow it, you can be the one to fill in this space.

5. Check the "Business Purpose" section of your sample agreement and make sure it includes the statement that indicates your company's purpose as engaging in lawful acts or activities for which an LLC may be formed.

You should also check the language in the "Term" section. "Indefinitely" is commonly used for the term.
In the terms of dissolution, "by a majority" is also commonly used.

6. You should also check the language in the "Management" section.

   A majority of small tutoring businesses are managed by the members as a whole, but you also have the option of getting managers for your tutoring business, especially if there are active and passive members.
   Whatever you decide, make sure your agreement contains the appropriate language as to how your company will operate.

7. Personalize the sample agreement by inserting the data from the notes you took as per Step 1 and Step 2. Be sure to include the necessary signature lines.

8. Print the agreement as well as a list of all members with their respective addresses and then staple them together.

   Let all members sign the agreement, have it photocopied, and then provide each member with a copy.

Be sure to keep the original somewhere safe and have additional copies in your files for reference.

Take note that this step-by-step guide does not constitute legal advice.

If there's anything about forming an LLC that you don't understand, it's still best to seek the advice of an attorney.

Online Tutoring

So, you've decide to start your very own tutoring business, but exactly what kind of tutoring business do you plan to set up?

Tutoring online is one option you may want to consider. Among its biggest benefits is that it makes the entire world your marketplace.

In fact, this is currently one of the online jobs that are gaining more and more value each day. Other than that, online tutoring can also be very rewarding.

There's currently a huge demand for tutors, especially since a huge number of companies all over the world are now outsourcing tutorial services to places where they can get excellent service at much lower charges.

The Internet has truly turned the whole world into a global village where even someone living halfway across the world can effectively tutor students from just about anywhere.

Modern technological tools have indeed made the previously impossible possible these days.

Of course, you can't just become an online tutor simply because you want to.

For starters, you'll have to possess the necessary knowledge and skills as dictated by the subject you plan to teach or the market you plan to serve.

You'll also need some basic knowledge on how to use the necessary equipment that'll help you carry out your online tutoring sessions.

Following is a discussion on the two ways of conducting online tutoring sessions:

1. Voice Over Internet Protocol (VOIP)

This tool allows you to talk with your student over the Internet with the use of speakers and microphones. It provides you with one of the easiest ways to carry out a conversation and discuss the subject you're teaching.

VOIP also makes it easy for you to understand your student's concerns and immediately address the areas of the subject he's having some difficulty with or is getting confused about.

In the same way, your student can quite easily ask you about something that's not quite clear to him.

And if you use a webcam with VOIP, then your tutoring sessions can achieve an even more realistic touch.

Carrying out your tutoring business in this manner makes it very similar to personal one-on-one instruction, since it allows you to use books, notes, diagrams, and other visuals as well.

2. Chat Technology

You're probably already aware of how online chatting works.

Well, an online chat tutoring session is exactly that:

Tutorials carried out through online chats.

This is the traditional form of online tutoring businesses. The drawback to this method is that it lacks the human touch and may not really allow you to explain every single aspect of the subject as clearly as you could in a face-to-face tutoring session.

Fortunately, there are some subjects that don't really need in-depth explanations, which makes them easy to teach via chat technology.

You can, of course, make your tutoring sessions more interesting by providing your student with some useful links where he can get in-depth explanations wherever necessary.

You can also make your sessions more interactive with the use of a webcam.

Now you know how to conduct a tutoring session online, but how exactly do you become an online tutor? Of course, you could venture out on your own, establish your own website, and market your tutoring services to your target market.

But, that may be too much of a hassle for a beginner like you. It may be a better idea for you to start out as an employee of any of the available websites offering online tutoring services.

Now you know how to conduct a tutoring session online, but how exactly do you become an online tutor? Of course, you could venture out on your own, establish your own website, and market your tutoring services to your target market.

But, that may be too much of a hassle for a beginner like you. It may be a better idea for you to start out as an employee of any of the available websites offering online tutoring services.

Here are the top ten companies you may want to seek employment with:

1. **Tutor.com** – The verdict for this website is that it offers great service and would definitely be a wise choice for students. The only drawback is the absence of an online chat option.

2. **eTutor** – The verdict is that the company offers competitive and outstanding services to their clients, although they don't have an online chat option.

3. **Tutorvista.com** – The verdict about this company is that they have a wonderful site that offers a great deal of help to students, although they can be a bit more expensive than other tutoring services.

4. **TutorNext** – The verdict is that the company appears to provide students with good basic tutoring services along with a lot of benefits and extras. The drawback is that their customer service doesn't really include that many options.

5. **eTutorworld** – The verdict is that this is one great tutoring company that can truly make a difference where a student's grades are concerned. The only drawback is that they don't accept check and PayPal payments.

6. **TutaPoint** – The verdict is that the company does offer a number of great features, but it's quite limited, since tutoring services are only available for three subjects: Science, Math, and Foreign Languages.

7. **Global Scholar** – The verdict is that this tutoring company does have some fairly good features, although it doesn't really live up to the other companies on this list. Plus, they could work some more on improving the security of their site.

8. **Vienova** – The verdict is that this company provides good basic tutoring services and excellent account tools. The drawback is that they don't provide information regarding payment methods and options.

9. **Sylvan Online** – The verdict is that this company may not be the best on this list, but it still provides fairly good tutoring services. The drawback is that their tutors are only available during particular times.

So, if you're serious about becoming a tutor, you might as well start checking for employment opportunities with the best online tutoring companies currently in operation.

Who knows, this just might provide you with the necessary knowledge and experience to venture out on your own.

How to Market Your
Tutoring Business

You've taken care of the first few steps towards establishing your own tutoring business. Now, you're probably wondering:

What's the best way for you to market your tutoring business and start getting students?

There are several marketing strategies you can choose from and you may even opt for a combination of these strategies in order to get the best results.

Marketing your new tutoring business probably ranks among the most challenging aspects of putting up a business venture, not to mention that it can also be the most fun.

You should, in fact, be excited about marketing your tutoring business. The main purpose of marketing a tutoring business is to let your target customers know that you exist and that you have a lot of benefits to offer them. To help you decide which marketing strategy would work best for your tutoring business, it may be a good idea to discuss each strategy in detail.

1. Business Cards

If you've ever been to a social event where you collected a few business cards from people whose business you were interested in, then you probably already understand the importance of having a good business card ready at all times.

You could meet potential clients (or their parents, if you're targeting young students) just about anywhere and it's definitely a good idea to always be ready to hand out your business cards. Your card will tell them what services you have to offer and how they can contact you should they find themselves in need of these services.

Of course, you'll have to make sure your business cards do what they're supposed to, which is to win clients for your tutoring business.

Add value to your business cards and ensure marketing success by using a catchy tagline that indicates a specific benefit clients can get from your business. Your cards should also look professional and up-to-date, and you should make sure they're always in good condition by placing them in a special case where they won't get dirty or bent.

2. Flyers

Advertising flyers have long been used as an effective marketing tool. They may be classified as a traditional form of advertising, but that doesn't necessarily mean they're outdated.

In fact, distributing flyers can be a very effective marketing strategy, provided you know how to use the flyers to your best advantage.

Perhaps the first thing you need to remember when creating flyers for your tutoring business is that a flyer is completely different from a business card.

The first thing you need to write on your flyer is a headline nobody can ignore. Once you've caught your target's attention with the headline, keep it by immediately raising a problem and then indicating that you have the solution to that problem.

Follow this up with a brief introduction of your tutoring business and an explanation of why hiring your services is something they *should* do.

For your closing statement, don't just give out your contact details. Instead, make a statement that calls for positive action and then offer a benefit, such as: "Enrol before (DATE) and get your first tutoring session for free!"

3. Word-of-mouth Advertising

This is, without doubt, the simplest and oldest form of advertising. It is also one of the most effective. However, it rarely becomes the focus of any advertising campaign. The reason for this may be the fact that it's almost impossible to predict or control what your target market will talk about.

The good news is that you actually stand a much better chance of effectively using word-of-mouth advertising these days, with the ever-growing popularity of social networking sites like Facebook and Twitter.

While people used to shy away from expressing their opinion about a product or service, today's social media generation is definitely very vocal about what they do and do not want.

To effectively use word-of-mouth to your advantage, be sure to always exude confidence about the kind of tutoring services you deliver. And whenever someone asks about your business, always address their inquiries in a courteous, knowledgeable, and sincere manner, regardless of whether you're talking in person, over the phone, or via e-mail.

Furthermore, you should be able to demonstrate the value of your tutoring services to your target customers. And in order to gain their trust, you should strive to be a good citizen of your community.

If people see that you're a good person worthy of their trust, they're more likely to refer your business to their family and friends.

4. Contacting Area Schools

For obvious reasons, schools within your area are the best sources of clients for your tutoring business.

Contact whoever's in-charge and ask permission to post advertising materials on school bulletin boards and distribute brochures, flyers, and business cards within school premises.

You may also ask for permission to distribute your resume to school teachers and counsellors for possible referrals. If any of the teachers or school staff are friends of yours, then it'll be a good idea to ask them for recommendations to students or their parents as well.

Schools also hold various events such as fairs where you could possibly rent a booth and promote your tutoring business. You may want to get a copy of the school calendar and make sure you're able to attend such events. There may even be occasions such as convocations where you could speak to students directly for a few minutes. Towards this purpose, it's important to establish a strong professional relationship with your area school authorities.

5. Local Publications

Also among the traditional forms of advertising, placing small ads in your local newspapers, magazines, and community newsletters can be one of the most inexpensive ways to start bringing in inquiries.
Make sure your ads clearly state your qualifications and that they can effectively sell your tutoring business. To make this strategy work, you'll have to learn a few facts about local publications.

For one thing, take note that a bigger number of individuals read local publications on a Sunday and they also spend more time reading on that day. It would do you good, therefore, to get your ads on the Sunday paper if you can't afford to let it run on a daily basis.

Take note as well that the keys to successful advertising on local publications are persistence and consistency.

So, if you decide to let your ad run on Saturdays and Sundays, make sure it runs on all Saturdays and Sundays of the month for a month or longer. You should also make sure you run the exact same advertisement every time.

A small ad that runs repeatedly without changing has a much better chance at success than a bigger ad that's seldom run or is changed from time to time. Repetition breeds familiarity over time and familiarity often breeds trust, which is vital for the success of a tutoring business.

6. Online Classifieds

Gone are the days when the term "classified ads" only referred to advertisements you run in newspapers and magazines.

These days, you have what's known as web-based classifieds, which are ads you run on the Internet and which can actually bring in a considerable amount of clients to your tutoring business.

Sites like Craigslist allow you to run online classifieds for free, making them the best places for you to start promoting your tutoring business to other web users. You also have the option of submitting your advertisement to online tutor directories like tutor-pages.com or tutor-ads.com.

Considering the fact that almost everyone is using the Internet in one way or another these days, online classifieds can indeed be one of the most cost-efficient ways for you to promote your tutoring business. To ensure success for your online classifieds, you'll need to identify your target audience and learn as much as you can about their Internet-use habits.

Furthermore, you'll have to test a few ads and then track their progress to determine which ad delivers the best results. When people search for products and services these days, they usually turn to the Internet. Therefore, when students or their parents search for good tutoring services, make sure they find you.

7. Tutoring Agencies

Draw up a list of all tutoring agencies within your area and then narrow them down to the ones with the most solid reputation and track record. Do some research to find out as much as you can about each agency on your list and then check the employment opportunities that may be available with them.

If you find one to your liking, then it may be a good idea to sign up with that particular tutoring agency and start your career as a tutor with them. You may then think about venturing out on your own once you've built a solid reputation for being a good tutor and a trustworthy individual.

8. College Career Opportunity Centres

These centres typically keep a list of all available jobs, including tutoring work. It can be a bit difficult to establish yourself as a reliable tutor if you venture out on your own immediately. Applying for a tutoring position with local centres is often a good start. These opportunity centres may even be a good source of referrals and help you build your initial customer base. In time, you should be able to build a reputation for being a trustworthy professional and word-of-mouth advertising should start working to your advantage

9. Creating a Brand

The kind of marketing message you convey to your target market is crucial when you market a new tutoring business. Even if you're selling exactly the same item as your closest competitor, you're more likely to come out on top of the competition if you're able to come up with better marketing strategies and if you can successfully create a brand for your company. Creating a brand for your company will make your tutoring business more valuable to potential customers.

Regardless of what type of business you're into branding is still important.

In fact, the more you create an attractive personality around your company brand, the more you set yourself apart from the competition, thus giving your tutoring business a much better opportunity for growth.

How do you know your brand is effective?
Simple. Market it to yourself.

Imagine that you're a would-be customer taking stock of a new player in the industry.

- Does the company brand look, sound, and feel authentic?

- Is it a fun and attractive brand?

Remember that marketing your tutoring business has to be fun, so don't take it too seriously. And even while you're working hard to create a brand, you should always remain true to yourself. That is what will make your brand truly authentic. And an authentic brand is something your competition can never take away.

In Conclusion...

Making a success out of a tutoring business involves not only a natural love for teaching and helping others, but also the ability to take proper care of the business end of the venture.

While it's important to make sure your students' needs are met at all times, it's equally important to stay organized and maintain good records in order to ensure the success of your tutoring business.

For the remainder of this section, we will assume that you'll be running your own tutoring business as opposed to seeking employment with a tutoring agency.

Among the things you need to do when running a tutoring business is to keep track of your income and expenses, and to make sure you follow all the applicable government regulations and guidelines, such as paying taxes on time.

It's advisable for you to keep your files in a specific box or drawer and assign categories for each file type so as to keep your documents well-organized at all times. It's also a good idea to keep a separate file for each of your students, indicating their names, addresses, contact numbers, and other pertinent information. You can use these files for personal use or when a colleague asks for references.

You may also want to consider setting aside a shelf on your bookcase to place all of your reference books and reading materials on tutoring, becoming a good tutor, running a tutoring business successfully, and other related topics.

You'll also probably have textbooks and other materials on the subjects you'll be tutoring. It's advisable to keep all these materials together for handy reference.

Like many other people, you may want to start your career as a tutor by working for a tutoring agency in order to gain the necessary experience and build a good reputation before venturing out on your own. I

f this is the case, then you'd do well to learn about how the agency handles billing and collections as well as the other aspects of a tutoring business.

Learning the ins and outs of the business while gaining experience and building your reputation helps you become all the more ready to set out on your own in the future.

Some points to remember

You've decided to start a tutoring business – for that you should be commended.

But, because this is your first time to start any kind of business, you're probably not quite sure how to go about it.

It can be easy to achieve success in this venture, but first you'll need to define what your specific goals are.

After all, success is defined simply as achieving your goals. Therefore, you can only truly measure your success if you've set precise and clear goals for yourself and your tutoring business.

In setting your business goals, you may want to ask yourself the following questions:

- Do I want to spend more time with my family?

- Do I want to earn around a hundred dollars each week?

- Do I want to start earning money simply by working at my personal computer?

- Do I want to help students feel better about themselves?

- Do I want people to truly appreciate me for the services I deliver?

- Do I want to turn my tutoring business into a full-time endeavour?

The decision as to what you want to achieve with your very own tutoring business is yours alone to make.

But, the good news is that as soon as you've decided on your business goals, the actual experience of working towards achieving these goals can be a lot of fun.

Not only will you earn a pretty good income from the business, but you'll also be making a significant amount of difference in the lives of both your students and their parents, especially if you deliver top-notch services.

Aside from knowing the purpose of your tutoring business, you'd also do well to decide beforehand where you plan to hold your tutoring sessions.

Would it be best for everyone concerned if the student came to your house or would it be much better for you to go to their house instead?

Another option you may want to consider is that of booking a room at the local library, which is usually free of charge, or perhaps you could meet with your students at a nearby college or university. Wherever you decide to hold your sessions, make sure there's a specific spot where you can talk quietly with your student without being disturbed.

If your business caters to very young students, then you should be prepared for parents requesting you to hold the tutoring sessions at their residence at least for the first few times.